Engaging Your Board:

It's Raining Yen

Kayte Connelly

BookLocker.com, Inc.
2011

First Edition

ACKNOWLEDGEMENTS

Much of these writings are based on the principles of MasterStream ® and practiced by graduates of Tension Management Institute. The nature of change starts with the premise that "human beings are not resistant to change."

T. Falcon Napier, founder of the MasterStream® method, expounds that "Human beings are resistant to losing control." By paying attention to productive levels of tension, control is sustained and energies can be directed towards industrious results.

You will see many references to tension management, and ChangeWorks® throughout these writings. Much of this work was previously written for the Philadelphia Women's Journal and is compiled here with additional thoughts and worksheets.

I would like to recognize all of the volunteers with whom I have ever worked in one capacity or another. I would like to thank those individuals with whom I have shared long and hard inquiries into the nature of human behavior and why individuals behave a certain way.

I would like to thank my parents, Neil and Cecelia for teaching us to find our voices; my siblings Cecelia Anne, Mary Margaret, Patricia Eileen, Susan Elizabeth, Jeanne Theresa, John Edward, Eileen Marie, Beth Maureen, Neil O'Boyle Jr. (and to the memory of Michael Hugh's short existence) for forcing the art of conversation. When it was your time to talk at the dinner table, you spoke loudly, quickly and tried to get out all of your thoughts in a controllable manner. I am constantly reminded of my humanity and my innate ability to ask 5 questions in a row before I give anyone a chance to answer one of them. Hence, there comes unto me a moniker of "questioneer." (*Imagine a hat with two question marks instead of mouse ears.*)

To T and the team at Tension Management Institute; to Deborah JH Bertolet, Pat Buchanan, Dale Mahle and John McKowen, thank you for your invaluable assistance and friendships.

Finally, my love, Marc Pratt Riddell, who never tires of my incessant questions, I am forever yours and look forward to our lasting conversations about perpetual change in our community.

Table of Contents

Introduction

Forty some years ago, my Grandmother, Cecelia Anne Colonel Qualter, a Church Lady, taught me how to type business letters asking local companies for items for the annual bazaar. Gramma, the sixth of 10 children, was adept at asking and guided me *"spell all of the names right – the first time. Let them know exactly what you want, when you want it, and what it will be used for upon its receipt. Then, thank them as many times in as many ways as you can."*

Good advice then; great advice now.

The difference is today, there are more than 1.8 million nonprofits that are registered with the IRS. That does not include our churches, authorities and other governmental bodies. They are all asking for the same dollars to support their mission.

It does not get easier. Communities continue to evolve. Interested individuals, many passionate about causes, become board members. Others join boards because of their jobs and they become a company representative. Or some because they believe that it is good for their image to be on a board.

Some nonprofits exist; some thrive; some flourish. The economy falters, government contracts dry up, budgets are cut, and distress ensues. People are upsized, down-sized, right sized, wrong sized in their jobs; contributions are reduced. Fewer volunteers want more meaningful, short-term positions; some board members question their roles.

This book is for those lucky boards. It is for the organizations that have well intended individuals wanting to do the right thing but they do not know how. It is for the boards who want to take purposeful action to move their organizations forward. It is for staff members who are seeking guidance on how to motivate their boards.

It is not a book on specific leadership trends. It is a classical set of expectations that board members should anticipate; how those expectations should be communicated; and how folks will be held accountable to fulfill those expectations.

While there has been a broad brush swathed across these experiences; the names have been changed to protect the guilty.

It is a book fostering lifelong learning, suggesting best practices and encouraging others to give themselves permission to hope, to try things a different way, to make mistakes and to laugh.

Doctors take the Hippocratic Oath: *first, do no harm.* Board members, volunteers and nonprofit staff should abide by that as well and then, and only after that commitment, use this guide to help you focus on your mission and your fiduciary responsibility.

Money does not flow like manna from heaven when you gain your charitable status. If you permit individuals to do their jobs by empowering them, they can become rainmakers for the best of causes no matter the size of the population it serves.

While I believe that many boards function well with strategic thinkers, most boards with whom I have worked seek support on some of the tactical maneuvering. I am often reminded by peers that "not all board members are entrusted to raise funds."

Blessed are the few for they shall inherit – or shall they?

As the mission would dictate, I believe most Chief Executives would prefer a board that understands the ramifications of good, solid fundraising principles and would not shirk from their responsibilities to give, get or get off with their time, talent or treasure.

Give me a board any day that knows the difference and strives diligently to perform in the best interest of the organization at hand.

-1-

A Nonprofit Preamble

We, the members of the nonprofit community, do solemnly pledge to do our best to uphold the rights and responsibilities of being a good charitable organization. We promise to do our duty and gain the knowledge and understanding of Charitable Laws to serve our clients.

As board members we will set policy and assume fiduciary responsibility, raise funds, and place reasonable expectations on qualified, compensated staff, when we are able to hire them.

As staff, we will keep ourselves and our board members current on best practices and trends, execute said policy and perform the administrative duties to the extent of our physical capability.

As stakeholders, whether individuals or corporate, we will support the mission of the organization through participation to the extent permitted.

We will do our utmost to uphold our duties, to be transparent in our actions and to embrace the respect of the public by remaining true to our mission and accountable to fellow citizens in these United States for whom we have been entrusted.

We perform all of these actions, with those benefiting from our mission in mind and recognize that we are neither bigger than the cause nor above reproach by the law.

** The term charitable refers to any organization eligible to receive a tax deductible donation.

HOMEWORK: Read this aloud at the start of each board meeting as you recite your mission and any other oaths or pledge your board members subscribe to upon accepting their roles.

AFFIRMATION: (Are Y-O-U 100% Committed?)

I AM a better board member.

-1A-

Ownership

The question often arises as to who "owns" a nonprofit.

Quite simply, the public owns it. The IRS has granted a nonprofit its status based on one of 28 different qualifications.

The purpose of this book is not to tell you how or why you received the status that you did. Go to www.stayexempt.org for your personal clarification.

The board of directors in many ways acts as owners on behalf of the public to achieve the mission of the organization.

In fulfilling its fiduciary responsibility, the board takes under advisement recommendations to serve the population for which the mission has defined said organization's purpose.

The board therefore, must act as if they are the owners. They bear responsibility for programs gone array or volunteers wreaking havoc within their purview.

It is when board members fully appreciate their responsibilities that they function well, tending to matters pertinent to the organization and achieving mission related goals.

HOMEWORK: Spend time at your next board meeting talking about the "ownership" of the organization.

AFFIRMATION: (Are Y-O-U 100% committed?)

I AM a better board member.

NOTES TO SELF:

GOALS: SMARTE$T

Specific: Who, what, when, where, why and how?	
Measurable: How much, how many?	
Acceptable: to those achieving the goals: attitudes, abilities, skills and $$.	
Realistic: Reflect on previous success and identify optimum conditions to be successful.	
Timely: There is a sense of urgency to accomplish now.	
Extending: Growing the capabilities of those charged with the goals.	
$$$$: What is the cost of accomplishing this goal? What is the cost of not accomplishing this goal?	
Test: Thoroughly appraise any additional changes for each goal through this process. Evaluate for successes and modify if necessary.	

-2-

7 Limiting Beliefs of Nonprofits

One of life's greatest frustrations may be taking charge of your destiny as the leader of a nonprofit organization. Many individuals and consequently, the organizations they may come to lead, get stuck in their path to success. They mire in self-doubt, in self-sabotaging behaviors, and never truly reach their goals.

Could this be you?

If so, you may be suffering from limiting beliefs. These are your core values that put the brakes on your progress. They present resistance to your goals and stop you dead in your tracks. They could cripple you and your performance.

Limitations prevent you from moving forward. They may cry from a spot deep down inside you that have been lingering for years. "Stop. Don't go there. I don't know how it will turn out."

We wrestle with ourselves. We can be our own worst enemies. We pin ourselves down on the mat with all of the things that we have carried forward in our beliefs system.

We listen to the language that rolls around us. "They said," "Statistics demonstrate," or "if you try...then this will happen." Who said that all of those things are true? Do we ever challenge who is the "we"? Has that been our experience as well?

Oftentimes, without realizing it, you may be facing an erroneous assumption about your own capabilities. Take this short quiz giving yourself a score of 1 for every "sounds like me/us", 2 for every "not recently."

HAVE YOU EVER FOUND YOURSELF SAYING?	SOUNDS LIKE US/ME	NOT RECENTLY
1. Why change? Things are fine the way they are.		
2. That won't work. We've already tried that.		
3. We can't do that.		
4. There's no money to do that.		
5. We don't have the time.		
6. We do not know how to do it.		
7. We simply do not have the resources.		
TOTALS:		

A score of 8 – 14 would be indicative of an open mind and probably a more imaginative form of leadership. A score of 1 – 7 would be indicative of someone suffering with severe limiting beliefs.

Examine these 7 key limiting beliefs for nonprofit leaders. Have you found yourself struggling with any of these situations for any specific task? Ever?

Here are some ways to identify empowering behaviors to overcome them.

1. Procrastination: Inability to get your job done. Either there are too many distractions from others because you haven't set boundaries or you are not holding yourself accountable.

Solution: Identify a solid list of tasks with levels of importance first and then urgency. Just because someone screams the loudest, doesn't mean you should pay attention to them first. You are rewarding abuses of power. Make a date with yourself to do what needs to be done to accomplish your tasks or delegate them to others.

2. **Epidemics of Self-doubt**: If there's something you don't like about yourself, it's better to hide it

than express it or explore it. Have you ever said "I can't; I'm too scared; I don't know enough; I'm not skilled enough? I have to fake it to make it."

Solution: Engage yourself productively in exercises that permit you to acknowledge your strengths and gain the confidence that you need to overcome your challenges. Identify and then, conquer your fears. Give yourself permission to do what you need to do to get it done.

3. **Perfectionism.** "If I don't do everything and do it right, I will end up alone." Doing the right thing should take precedence. Are you guilty of micromanaging? Do you watch every detail instead of the big picture?

Solution: Delegate, delegate, delegate and empower yourself and those around you by giving them the opportunity to excel. Give yourself a break and others permission to make mistakes.

Again, what is the big picture and are you losing sight of your goals because you are focusing on minutiae instead of the vision? Does it have to be done 100% of your way? Would the job be acceptable if it was 80% complete?

4. **Scarcity:** Repeat after me. "I cannot earn a living doing something I like. We can't make money because we are nonprofit. We are not allowed to look successful because then, no one will give us money."

   Does your organization look like a loser? Is it dirty, sloppy? Do guests have a clean place to sit while waiting? How long until you get a live person on the phone?

   Do not believe for one minute that folks will give money to an organization that does not appear to be well managed. No one wants to throw money into an endless pit where progress is not easily recognized.

Solution: Clean up your act. Start behaving like a professional organization and one that welcomes abundance. Acknowledge that you are a winner and act like one.

5. **I'm too busy**. I don't have enough time, money, staff, etc.

Solution: Time management skills may help you realize other benefits. Are you a wheel in constant motion, afraid to let anyone help you? Trusting in others, permitting them to make mistakes, and delegating may all prove beneficial to your end results.

Learn to prioritize; set deadlines and block out time for the things you need to do. Every day, everything on your plate cannot be number one.

6. **I'll fail** despite all of the hard work. If I fail, I should feel bad for a very long time and then be scared to try again. Often leaders burn through a

vast majority of resources including their staff. They find themselves stuck in a hamster wheel doing the same thing over and over again. Or they believe, "if I am successful, no one will like me."

Solution: Assess your strengths and weaknesses. Surround yourself with others that bring you balance. Hire people smarter than you are. Find board members with specific skills. Delegate to others whose skills set compliments your specific needs.

7. **I'll never.....**What are your goals? If you truly believe that you will never, you never will – no matter how you complete the sentence.

Solution: Set goals; know what you want. Build roads to get there. Find out what it takes and do it. Reflect on what you want and go after it.

If you release your mind and dispel these myths, you will overcome these limitations and set your goals and that of your organizations on an unlimiting path to success.

HOMEWORK:

Go through the 7 limiting beliefs. Decide which of these you may be guilty of and what you plan to do about it.

Start small so you will reach successes. Build upon those successes until you have overcome what is holding you back.

AFFIRMATION: (Are Y-O-U 100% Committed?) *Therefore, today, I AM committed to this goal. Everything that I do will be driven by this goal. I will not permit interruptions until I have completed it. OR, I will make more time in my life to bring balance into it.*

NOTES TO SELF:

GOALS: SMARTE$T

Specific: Who, what, when, where, why and how?	
Measurable: How much, how many?	
Acceptable: to those achieving the goals: attitudes, abilities, skills and $$.	
Realistic: Reflect on previous success and identify optimum conditions to be successful.	
Timely: There is a sense of urgency to accomplish now.	
Extending: Growing the capabilities of those charged with the goals.	
$$$$: What is the cost of accomplishing this goal? What is the cost of not accomplishing this goal?	
Test: Thoroughly appraise any additional changes for each goal through this process. Evaluate for successes and modify if necessary.	

-3-

Proudly Providing Disciplined Leadership

In his monograph accompanying his book *Good to Great*, Jim Collins throws this premise to the world of leadership. "Mediocre companies rarely display the relentless culture of discipline that we find in truly great companies. A culture of discipline is not a principle of business; it is a principle of greatness."

If you believe that, and you believe that the social sector has within its business model the opportunity to become great, then you believe that the leadership in nonprofits also has the potential to demonstrate greatness.

There are many informational resources available to propel potential leadership into the forefront. John Maxwell has his golden rules. Rudy Guliani suggests bravery and hope; Colin Powell, the power of optimism.

I refer to all of these when called upon to present classes or coach groups surrounding this vital missing link. ChangeWorkers® like me, find our base in leadership teachings in the work of T. Falcon Napier and his theories about Pride-based Leadership vs. Shame-based Leadership.

Think about these questions surrounding your leadership style and determine how you are able to engage those whom you serve in their optimum performance. Reflect on the evidence that you have to demonstrate the truth in your answer.

1. Are your workers fearlessly following your leadership?

2. Do you put paperwork before people work?

3. Do you understand the productivity triggers of each of your employees?

4. Have you had formal leadership training or are you mimicking the traits of the so-called leaders before you?

5. Have you optimized employee engagement so they easily adapt to work culture changes?

6. Do you have power, authority, status and access of a supposed leader but still lack influence?

Leaders who are intentional about doing what is right for their organizations engage themselves and their subordinates in a continual reflection of their outcomes.

When organizational goals are set, who is setting them? Do you align your resources with the desired time frames in which the goals are to be accomplished? How can one be expected to accomplish extraordinary goals if the time, money and skills are not there to support them?

Do you engage in disciplined thought and take disciplined action? Do you permit your team to be engaged in disciplined thought and action? How do you know this to be true?

Great leaders inspire others to act. Let me repeat that.

Great leaders inspire others to act.

They have a passion that is contagious and they make it their business to be pragmatic in their approach. Movement is measured in increments and individuals are held accountable for their participation.

If you think about no other facet to being a great leader and concentrate on pride-full passionate discipline, could your team become more engaged in the accomplishments of your organization?

For example: identify all of the members of your team and ask yourself how are you holding them all accountable? Does your board do what is expected of them? How do you know this to be true? What can you do as a leader, to support them in your expectations?

Do your staff members and volunteers do what is expected of them? How do you know this to be true? What can you do as a leader, to support them in your expectations?

Are you as their leader, consistent and approachable to support others on your team in the accomplishments of your expectations?

T. Falcon Napier espouses that Pride-based Leaders clearly define their expectations and hold others accountable.

Further, Pride-based Leaders do not change the message when approaching their respective teams. They are consistent in their communiqué.

The constancy of the message is what provides the discipline. The consistency of communications is what drives the message. The message is the goal and the clear expectations to achieve the goal are constant and consistent.

Communications are delivered in a personal manner. Accomplishments are celebrated in a personal manner. The Pride-based Leader inspires others to actions because they respect the individual as a single contributor who has a poignant role in the success of the organization.

Should a time come when expectations are not met, the Pride-based Leader discusses the situation privately. Never is one scolded in a room of other individuals. This leader encourages solutions and empowers others to greatness and is not selfish in sharing acknowledgements with their team.

Look within your organization; look within your spirit. Are you the one who has the power to transform your organization to one of greatness or will you remain mediocre?

As Jim Collins states, our world is full of mediocrity. The greatness of leadership is not monopolized by business. Nor is the dearth of leadership.

I would suggest that the social sector has greatness within its capacity if it permits itself to be purposeful, persistent and full of pride.

HOMEWORK:

Name three leadership qualities that you admire in other individuals with whom you work.

How can you emulate them?

How are your communications being received?

Do you need to change anything about your leadership style?

AFFIRMATION: (Are Y-O-U 100% Committed?) *Today, I AM committed to spending 15 minutes to reflect on my leadership abilities.*

NOTES TO SELF:

GOALS: SMARTE$T

Specific: Who, what, when, where, why and how?	
Measurable: How much, how many?	
Acceptable: to those achieving the goals: attitudes, abilities, skills and $$.	
Realistic: Reflect on previous success and identify optimum conditions to be successful.	
Timely: There is a sense of urgency to accomplish now.	
Extending: Growing the capabilities of those charged with the goals.	
$$$$: What is the cost of accomplishing this goal? What is the cost of not accomplishing this goal?	
Test: Thoroughly appraise any additional changes for each goal through this process. Evaluate for successes and modify if necessary.	

-4-

Selective Board Enrollment

It never fails to amaze me when people say, "I could never try that with my board. My board doesn't know what they are supposed to be doing."

Or, here's another one: "I can't get Mr. Fill-in-the-blanks off the board. He provided the endowment. He's a fixture. He won't let us move forward."

Sound eerily familiar?

Why do you think that is?

I recall the first time when I was approached by a fellow board member who asked me, "Have you thought about who it is you want to serve next on the board?"

I was taken aback. Here I was, 14 years into my career, a Chief Executive, and it was the first time someone asked me that question. Usually the newest board members came from a contributor; a friend of a friend; or someone who had been a loyal committee member who out performed others.

Never did I think that I could have any input into who would be the next board member. Yet, why is that?

When we hire staff, don't we look for a specific skill set and evidence of accomplishments? Why should it be different for a board member?

What do your by-laws say about the composition of your board? Do you need a certain number of members to be in compliance? When is the last time you looked at your by-laws to see if you are in compliance? Have you been conducting business within the confines of your definition for a quorum?

By-laws are created for a purpose. They are crafted in such a way to accommodate change. They reflect certain flexibilities for the growth or shrinkage of an organization so it may continue its existence with minor tweaking.

Do you need 30 people to support the guidance and advisement for a $50,000/year operating budget? That might be extreme. But, if you have a $5 million budget, managing 30 might pose a set of different circumstances.

We are not here to debate the size of your board.

What we are here to do is to consider the optimum skills and other pre-requisites needed to accomplish the goals for your organization.

From the beginning here are questions to consider when making your selection of community members to best serve your mission.

1. Do you have a board application form? Similar to a job application, it should contain pertinent achievements for the individual such as education, employment, former community service, understanding of the organization's mission and any other items you might think appropriate.

2. Some boards consider diversity reflecting the composition of the clientele served so age, race and sex may be factors. If that is your intention, an application can greatly facilitate that part of the process.

I would encourage you to make sure that if you are bringing a woman on the board, to be confident that this is the best woman for such service. Or, if you are bringing a male into a predominantly female organization, then he should be bringing the best of skills with him.

I often hear tales of individuals who were selected and brought onto boards because they filled a diversity quotient. When that individual falls short of expectations for whatever reason, it can cause considerable harm to the organization because of lack of planning and foresight.

3. Other aspects might be geography or residencies in specific neighborhoods. Again, your mission might dictate that; or it might not.

4. At a minimum, you would want to have representation from the professions that make a community whole. The number of representatives could vary. But a homogenous board, no matter what the flavor, seldom moves forward.

Imagine if you will, a board of all bankers with financial backgrounds running an organization whose primary focus was educational programs.

Or how would a group of elementary school educators shepherding a credit union adequately reflect the desired expertise?

You might want to consider someone with an accounting background, an attorney, a business person, a clergyman, or a clinician (if it's relevant). Further, you may want an educator, someone from government, a justice representative (in addition to an attorney, if relevant) and perhaps even another representative from a nonprofit organization. How about the ever nebulous "community-at-large" seats, or a youth representative, or a client representative?

The more of your community that you have represented that can accomplish the job as a board member, the less time you will be faced with the dreaded *"if onlies:"* If only we had this, or *if only* we had so and so. Intentional selection provides a well rounded guidance group and minimizes wasted time with speculation.

5. Finally, you would want to delve deeper into their proficiency and look for advisors that brought the expertise that you needed to accomplish your goals.

Who has advertising expertise, or can support administrative systems? General business, budgeting or financial backgrounds are also areas that are typically sought.

Community contacts are a huge factor that is often coupled with fundraising. Legal, marketing and planning are crucial as are program, public relations and volunteer management.

Again, reflecting your specific needs you might consider social work.

ALWAYS, always consider those that have demonstrated exemplary board leadership (serving as an officer) within other organizations.

As your process is defined, you would want to consider the interviewing process and most important, checking of references.

When you perform these functions with the due diligence of any other fiduciary responsibility, you can be assured of some return on your time investment.

Can you count the number of board member "mistakes" who were ill-fitted for your organization and wreaked havoc while warming a seat? Can you afford to thoughtlessly distribute the future of your organization into the hands of the inept?

I have been reminded by others that not every board member is a well intended individual citizen who is passionate about your cause. Believe it or not, some prevail upon the kindness of others to advance their own agendas or to fulfill their work obligation to represent a certain business or sponsor.

Too often the harm is done leaving carnage behind the wrath of the board member who serves his or her own agenda.

A good governance committee will reflect the composition of the board, regularly report on expectations and fulfillment and keep each other in check. A simple tool can afford them ease with which to perform this essential function.

Applications, interviews and reference checks are basics for board servitude. If it's "too complicated" for some individuals, then maybe that is the fallout an organization must suffer to assure their mission is being satisfied within reason. Let them self-select out of the process just as they would a job.

If someone survives initial scrutiny, and has passion for the mission, it gives you additional leverage.

Boards that just take anybody deserve whomever they get.

FROM THE OTHER SIDE:

Here are things to consider if you are asked to serve on a board of directors. Before you do anything, check your passion temperature about the organization.

If it doesn't feel like a mission you can fall in love with, then do everyone a favor and don't get involved.

An invitation to serve on a board carries equal if not more scrutiny. You have a right to be concerned about the position.

As a potential board member, you may ask to see what you are getting yourself into – just as you would a job.

Under strict confidentiality ask to see:

- A job description
- The current board roster
- The strategic plan
- Current program of work

- Committee structure/roster/description
- Financials including last year's annual report; last month's report and the most recent audit
- Copy of the most recent board meeting minutes
- Any and all printed materials including newsletters, fundraising collateral, etc.

If you are lucky enough to be interviewed, inquire about D & O insurance. Program and evaluation processes could also be included as well as any strategic alliances.

True, very true, that many of these answers may not be thought of as intricately involved with setting policy or fiduciary responsibility.

Just because an organization can produce any or all of these documents and also has a series of interviews does not indicate that they are necessarily well managed. But, it would give a clearer picture of what to expect and diminish a good number of questions that might be rolling around in your head about said organization.

HOMEWORK:

Pull your by-laws out and read the piece about board composition. Are you in compliance? If not, what do you have to do to get in compliance? Are they so dated that you need a by-law revision?

Make a chart with your Governance Committee to assure the talent that you need is represented. If not, why not? How long will it take you to reach optimum representation? What/who are the obstacles? How can you surmount them?

AFFIRMATION: (Are Y-O-U 100% Committed?) *Today, I AM more strategic about the selection of board members.*

NOTES TO SELF:

GOALS: SMARTE$T

Specific: Who, what, when, where, why and how?	
Measurable: How much, how many?	
Acceptable: to those achieving the goals: attitudes, abilities, skills and $$.	
Realistic: Reflect on previous success and identify optimum conditions to be successful.	
Timely: There is a sense of urgency to accomplish now.	
Extending: Growing the capabilities of those charged with the goals.	
$$$$: What is the cost of accomplishing this goal? What is the cost of not accomplishing this goal?	
Test: Thoroughly appraise any additional changes for each goal through this process. Evaluate for successes and modify if necessary.	

-5-

Connecting the Dots

Once a year, a board orientation should be conducted. Usually it is held before the first board meeting. New board members, or those seeking refreshers, are brought together to review key components of their rights and responsibilities as a critical decision maker.

1. The primary duty of any board member is to direct policy. The fiduciary obligations encumbered through said policy direct the initiatives and programs that will be undertaken in any given year.

Policy has anything to do with spending. Just like the policies initiated through our Congressional or State offices, there are two aspects to setting policy.

One is setting the policy – or legislating it. The second is appropriating the funds to allow the program to exist.

In other words, yes, you will be involved in setting a budget for the programs delivered in the next fiscal year. More importantly, yes, you will be expected to understand and support the manner in which the organization raises funds to deliver said programs.

Y-O-U are responsible to assure the organization is financially stable.

Board members that understand those key processes and only those board members should be permitted to continue through the orientation.

2. Then, the pertinent facts and statistics should be presented through a review of the organization's compelling history.

A review of the by-laws is imperative.

What were the beginning phases? Who were the key architects/funders, for example? Where did we come from? What have we done? What are we doing now? How much does it cost to do that? Where do we get the money from?

All of these are great questions that should b answered during the orientation.

3. One might consider reviewing key policies and procedures and have obligatory forms such as Conflict of Interest and/or Confidentiality signed. This is a great opportunity for questions to be asked and answered about ethical considerations for each member.

Signing those documents at this time can also be interpreted as business as usual and should set the stage for permitting questions to be asked whenever they arise.

Better to have inquiries encouraged and receive responses than having someone claim "I didn't know."

Have you ever heard a longstanding board member reflect, "Oh, that's what you meant? Well if I knew that was what you meant, I never would have voted for it."

The balance of the orientation agenda should be the facts and figures that anyone entrusted with any responsibilities should expect.

4. Prepare a who's who. Who are the staff members? What do they do? Do you have an organizational chart? Does the organizational chart also define how the staff is paid, for example? Which grants support which programs and consequently, which staff?

How about fellow board members? Where are they from? How do I contact them? What are the committees? How is committee selection determined? Is there an organizational chart? Who are the officers?

5. It's time to review the financials. A copy of last year's audit and/or your 990 should be reviewed allowing plenty of time for questions and answers.

Last year's budget and end of the year comparisons, as well as this year's budget must be presented with equal detail and time allotment for Q & A.

6. There should be a basic board protocol introduced at this point. Review the preparation of your board agenda and how one might bring an item for consideration to the board.

Do you use a consent agenda, for example, which would permit an extended allotment of time to discuss critical issues or permit additional board training?

Do you use Roberts Rules?

How do issues percolate from the committees up to board discussion? How the committee work drives the budget could bring in another opportunity to discuss the financials and their importance.

7. Committee assignments could be distributed complemented with obligations for service. How many board meetings must one attend? How many committee meetings?

Making expectations perfectly clear permits better communication and provide the foundation for better service from your respective board members.

8. A calendar of other critical programs or events would assure attendance. Examples might be: your annual meeting, your big fundraiser, or graduation from one of your programs.

Wouldn't it be wonderful to provide information to your board members well in advance to allow them to commit for those important dates?

9. The Individual Board Plan™ will have a chapter devoted entirely to itself. This would also be a critical piece of the overall orientation. If necessary, provide time during the orientation to fill out this document within the respective teams.

10. Continuous Review – To complete the orientation, the systems used to evaluate the proceedings of the board and the organization should be disclosed.

Does your organization go through an accreditation process, for example? Is there a professional designation that depicts accomplishment of certain types of standards?

How does the organization perform its self-evaluation? How do you know the impact of your services?

I am often asked if all of this paperwork is really necessary. Does it matter if you receive an accreditation or you hold yourself accountable to attaining specific goals?

I promise you, "Yes. It matters." It demonstrates to your funders that you are serious about managing their money. It affords your client's the best service possible. It conveys to your community that you are serious about the way you conduct your affairs.

Any conversations with your board members, any information that can support them in doing the job that you expect will afford your clients the benefits of having a job well done and a thriving organization.

HOMEWORK: Comprise an agenda for your next board orientation. What do you need to create to direct a logical path for your board to follow for this year? Answer the questions contained in this chapter.

AFFIRMATION: (Are Y-O-U 100% Committed?)

I AM providing a clear path for the board to follow.

Repeat this again with much more gusto:

I AM providing a clear path for the board to follow.

NOTES TO SELF:

GOALS: SMARTE$T

Specific: Who, what, when, where, why and how?	
Measurable: How much, how many?	
Acceptable: to those achieving the goals: attitudes, abilities, skills and $$.	
Realistic: Reflect on previous success and identify optimum conditions to be successful.	
Timely: There is a sense of urgency to accomplish now.	
Extending: Growing the capabilities of those charged with the goals.	
$$$$: What is the cost of accomplishing this goal? What is the cost of not accomplishing this goal?	
Test: Thoroughly appraise any additional changes for each goal through this process. Evaluate for successes and modify if necessary.	

-6-

The Individual Board Plan™

The Individual Board Plan™ (IBP™) is a process I developed when I was designing my business model. There was a commonality among most of the boards which I led or served.

Oftentimes, there is a large disconnect between what the board's expectations are, and the expectations of the staff.

In late summer 2006, shortly after I had returned from the Better Business Bureau (or Wise Giving Alliance) training on standards for charities, I sat down and thought about all of the activities a board member should become familiar with to be the very best board member they could be.

If I had a well rounded board, they would know which aspects of the organization that pertained strictly to the business of the board.

Not so surprisingly, I came up with a list of 345 activities that surrounded categories such as: board development; committee development; membership; programs and services; communications; financial reporting; and human resource management.

There are probably activities that I did not include. Some folks are a bit put off when they review it. If you'd like a copy, they are available through the website.

The instructions were straightforward. Simple answers were yes, no, maybe and I don't know. It wasn't meant to be pass/fail but to discern the areas of your organization where strengths were lacking.

The scoring suggested an interesting array of rankings.

Add up your scores for each page. Add up the collective page score. (6 pages)

Perfect score = 345   Excellent score = 300 – 345
Good score = 250 – 299   Okay score = 200 – 249
Needs Improvement = 150 – 199
Needs Great Attention = 100 – 149
Think about turning your money over to another
organization = 50 – 99
Stop right now/close your doors/turn it over = 0 – 49

Okay, so here's just another assessment, right?

No, not really. What I do with that tool, is to offer a different type of strength finder, one where board members can define for themselves where they might flex their muscles and where there is definitely some need for improvement.

It is all dependent on what you expect from fellow board members. It is also dependent on what you expect as a board member.

An organization chooses up to 25 activities, measures the ability, challenge and importance of each activity for each board member. Each activity is then separated on a ChangeGrid® and the levels of expertise someone has professed or could use some additional training in, is easily defined.

The ChangeGrid® suggests a path for committee placement based upon the answers. Each application is client-driven and activity specific, so it tends to draw a crystal clear trail for them to follow.

When you have a group of loyal individuals that gather to advise an organization to which they have pledged some loyalty, they cannot possibly all have the same strengths, or weaknesses.

Here are the 25 activities that I have crafted for the "Board Development" segment of the overall survey. Read them with care and extreme curiosity. This piece could be the start to your own board assessment.

1. Each board member is clear on the mission of the organization.
2. Each board member has received an orientation and understands how their expertise relates to their role as a board member.

3. Each board member understands their financial oversight obligations and the need to develop financial resources that will support the mission, its programs and strategies.
4. Every board member has reviewed the most current 990 and understands the impetus of our Sarbanes Oxley adopted policies.
5. Every board member acknowledges the need for transparency in the annual and regularly posted financial reports.
6. Board minutes are recorded, distributed in a timely manner, and approved.
7. There is an annual process to monitor and measure clear objectives for each committee.
8. Every board member's expertise is valued when attending board meetings.
9. There is a process to evaluate needed expertise and cultivate new board members who will balance the experience needed to fill identified gaps.
10. Every board member comes to meetings prepared and brings only board business to the table.
11. Every board member serves effectively on at least one committee.
12. Every board member acknowledges their financial obligation (personal pledge) and fulfills it regularly.
13. Every board member has signed a conflict of interest form.
14. Every board member has completed a board profile.

15. Every board member has agreed to attend educational forums about board responsibilities as they are deemed necessary.
16. There is a process to regularly assess the progress of the organization.
17. The board acknowledges the table of organization and supports the efforts of paid staff.
18. The board understands the difference between setting policy and administrative responsibilities.
19. Every board member demonstrates respect for the time at hand and the need to follow parliamentary procedure.
20. There are enough board members to complete our program of work.
21. We are engaged in the community as a whole.
22. We are respected in our field.
23. The board acknowledges compliance with all financial, funding and licensing requirements.
24. The board has the right representation of money, expertise and contacts.
25. The board has diverse community representation, including those recipients of our services.

Part B of the IBP™ is the accountability piece. Reflecting back on the budget for the year and the committee assignments, what role does each board member play and what will they commit to?

There are the perfunctory requirements that the board has set: e.g. as part of your board responsibility, you have to give a gift of some amount. Most boards stipulate a personal gift somewhere between $500 and $50,000. Some boards indicate that each board member must provide a personal gift that is "significant "to them, in addition to bringing in outside sources of revenue. The interpretation of significant is left to the individual. This is especially true with organizations that have clients or youth members represented.

(Never give a board member the option to "work off" their personal commitment – either through administrative or other gifts-in-kind. It brings a huge imbalance to the board when there is no personal stake in the game. And, you never want board members filing in your office or staffing your phones. Although well intended, you need a different caliber of individual to support your work and may find yourself open to micromanagement tendencies – but that is another book.)

Then, after the personal gift is secured (personal means written from your own checkbook and does not include outside gifts that are obtained), what else does each board member have to do within this fiscal year?

It could be selling so many tickets to the annual fundraiser. It could be securing a specific number of large sponsorships or new members. Whatever the expectations, write them down and have every board member commit to them by signing a document.

A crucial piece is asking the board members about their comfort level for bringing in additional dollars, members, sponsors, etc. Ask what they need to become more fluent in the "asking" language.

This permission for the board members to say, "I'm happy to help you, but I need some more training" is what helps one organization hurdle over others that may have the same rotation of board members.

As Executive Directors, Presidents or Chief Executive Officers we often hear, "I'll be on your board, but don't ask me to fundraise." Why do you think that is?

Could it be that they truly don't understand the concept? Have you considered that members of your board don't have the information they need to complete "the ask" in a way that would be meaningful.

The IBP™ is similar to an individual education plan because it contains the conversation surrounding board obligations and it gives people permission to grow into becoming a better ambassador for you and to think about fundraising in a different way.

When a person has a stake in the organization and the organization responds by saying "we will do all that we can to support you in acknowledging your weaknesses. Now, let's work together to get you stronger in that area," wonderful results occur.

By allowing the board members to be treated like any other human being and providing them with the resources they need to do the job, they will become more productive.

It is a rare occasion when a potential board member knows exactly what they are supposed to do for any given organization. Once someone reaches "expert" status, they are usually allied where other factors permit them to succeed.

The final piece to making the IBP™ process successful is to have the board members hold each other accountable through a committee of peers.

In the "old" days, there was a nominating committee that functioned by gathering names they put forward to fill vacant seats.

Or you might have a fossil or two, that came with money "in the beginning" that has served on the board since its inception and refuses to give up their seat.

The slate was proposed: maybe there was an interview; maybe references were checked; maybe there was an orientation; maybe there was a skills assessment and on a really great board, there might be an orientation.

I might suggest that the introduction of a system that spells out expectations with peers holding each accountable, provides a new stratum in the world of boards success stories.

Communicating a consistent message – "all board members must, should, can" and "we will help you to be triumphant" affords an organization a brighter picture than might have been formerly realized.

While an executive committee typically has a good pulse on the organization and its needs, the task of supervising the growth of your board could be assigned to a separate committee. That Governance, Board Engagement or whatever name you give it, committee, is then responsible for the annual check-in with fellow board members. (Does your Executive Committee want that task as well as the additional oversight of board business? Should only ONE committee really have all of that power? How does that allow for others to become engaged?)

That committee schedules time to review with each member, what the desired outcomes are and how they are expected to fulfill the budget.

It also helps to capture the energy from someone who is passionate about the organization and may tend to get off track if not directed.

HOMEWORK:

Think about what you need your board members to accomplish for you in a given year.

Find a champion or two that will support you in talking with fellow board members about the desired change.

Develop a plan of action that will support, not interfere with the intended change and back it with a timeline and anticipated costs for action.

AFFIRMATION: (Are Y-O-U 100% Committed?)

I AM permitting our board to be the best that it can be. I AM supporting the practice of holding each other accountable.

NOTES TO SELF:

GOALS: SMARTE$T

Specific: Who, what, when, where, why and how?	
Measurable: How much, how many?	
Acceptable: to those achieving the goals: attitudes, abilities, skills and $$.	
Realistic: Reflect on previous success and identify optimum conditions to be successful.	
Timely: There is a sense of urgency to accomplish now.	
Extending: Growing the capabilities of those charged with the goals.	
$$$$: What is the cost of accomplishing this goal? What is the cost of not accomplishing this goal?	
Test: Thoroughly appraise any additional changes for each goal through this process. Evaluate for successes and modify if necessary.	

-7-

The Chair Takes the Lead

"When you don't know where you are going, any road will take you there," a line from the Cheshire Cat in *Alice in Wonderland*.

Recently, this announcement was shared as an invitation for a nonprofit roundtable.

Has your board chair received any formal board chair leadership training or are they mimicking the lackluster performance of those before them? Has your governance committee reviewed the specific skills of your board and are you filling your vacant seats with intentional, well-thought out appointments?

There is an old nursery rhyme song called, "The Farmer in the Dell." As it goes on, there is an intentional selection among the individuals who stood up, lined up and were willing to play. The rules were fairly simple and anyone could play because they understood the game, how to participate and when it was over.

Have you ever departed from a board meeting wondering what you were doing there? Have you ever felt like you are finishing the line of the Farmer in the Dell "hi, ho, the dario" with the phrase "the chair takes the lead?"

Did you become the chair by default? Were you the last one standing when the rest of the group fell down?

What does it take to become the Chair? Who should be selected for this position? When will the "right" person be selected and how can that individual prepare for his or her successors?

In a 2009 study completed by the Center for Creative Leadership, individuals were asked to rank a number of competencies they felt were most critical to the success of their organization now and to the success of the organization five years in the future. The purpose of the study was to identify gaps or deficiencies in leadership talent.

Not so surprisingly, the same skills were placed in the top two positions for desired strengths of existing leaders and future leaders. They were: leading people and strategic planning.

Each chairman has the responsibility to lead people and to plan strategically. Each chairman has the ability to provide the board with an opportunity to revisit the rules of engagement, to sustain the vision (or create one if it hasn't happened), to establish boundaries, to assign and communicate expectations and to hold others accountable. Or not.

Have you experienced these components of leadership (see chapter 3) and can you confidently say, "that is the essence of all of our chairmen; of some of our chairmen; of none of our chairmen?"

So where are you going? How will you get there?

As I frequently hear, "no one else wanted the job so I got stuck with it...I want to make sure that this doesn't happen again."

This is the start of a great organization, one where the chair admits "we need to move forward. Things aren't right. Let's do what is necessary to get back on track and back to mission."

This Chairman will assure that there is continuity in the flow of the board. They will inspire others to do their work. They will foster camaraderie as the committees execute their assignments. They will lead the charge to devise emergent systems for the board to grow in its job meaningfully.

What do you do if this happens to you? What if you are the one who suddenly becomes the Chair and you do not have good stewards to model? How do you begin to transform the organization and instill succession planning at every step of the way?

The chair of the board has several specific responsibilities, separate and apart from the direct oversight for completing the annual and strategic plans; setting the budget and meeting financial goals; evaluating the Chief Executive and board; and leading the organization as the Chief Elected Official.

Here are twelve principles that will foster trust among strangers, create working relationships and an environment where work of the board is encouraged to be executed.

1. Know your fellow board members. Understand their strengths and their challenges.
2. Commit to providing all board members with the information they need to make decisions in a timely and efficient manner.
3. Reassure the board that they may ask questions about any policy decisions. In a congenial

community, team members feel comfortable enough to ask questions in any or all meetings.

4. Supply an atmosphere where individual board members are advocating for ideas to solve problems, not necessarily for adoption of their own proposals.

5. Instill in every board member a pride that is associated with what is accomplished.

6. Focus on development of some of the softer skills for serving on a board as well as encouraging some joviality.

7. Ensure that legal and ethical integrity are primary in all dealings.

8. Assure that operational decisions will be dedicated to staff within financial parameters.

9. No surprises. No recommendation from a committee, no presentation.

10. Thoughtfully prepare meetings using consent agendas where possible and outlining actions to be taken so the board can prepare itself.

11. Recognize energy levels. Put the heavy stuff at the front of your meeting. Hard decisions should never wait to be last on the agenda.

12. Remember to bring every conversation back to the mission. For example, if you are working with children, remember to ask – how will this discussion benefit the children at least every 15 minutes. If your mission supports a trade association, bring it back to the members.

These suggestions coupled with those from the next chapter should assure a bright future for your organization.

As the first chairman to be embarking on a new journey, it may not be possible to juggle all of these principles as you are committing to the work of the board.

Once there are precedents set, others will follow naturally in your footsteps. The unique partnership of a chairman leading change and supporting the Chief

Executive Officer in implementing new policies and procedures is sought after by few; accomplished by fewer.

HOMEWORK: Think about the behaviors you would like to see from your board chair. Think about the behaviors you would not like to see from your board chair.

Determine what you can do about assuring the desired behaviors and when you will implement these changes.

AFFIRMATION: (Are Y-O-U 100% committed?)

I AM supporting the board chair during their tenure.

NOTES TO SELF:

GOALS: SMARTE$T

Specific: Who, what, when, where, why and how?	
Measurable: How much, how many?	
Acceptable: to those achieving the goals: attitudes, abilities, skills and $$.	
Realistic: Reflect on previous success and identify optimum conditions to be successful.	
Timely: There is a sense of urgency to accomplish now.	
Extending: Growing the capabilities of those charged with the goals.	
$$$$: What is the cost of accomplishing this goal? What is the cost of not accomplishing this goal?	
Test: Thoroughly appraise any additional changes for each goal through this process. Evaluate for successes and modify if necessary.	

-8-

Establishing Trust in Action: 10 Tips for Productive Committee Meetings

Management in nonprofit organizations often entrusts a delegation of like-minded community volunteers to support specific tasks to achieve an end result.

At such committee meetings, work should be meaningful, contain elements of problem-solving, decision making, and accountability through reporting. Towards that end, they should be purposeful and participatory.

Do you dread or look forward to committee meetings? Do you ever find yourself saying, "Why am I going to this meeting? Nothing ever gets done." Or the meeting becomes a platform for one, strong-willed person to dominate and control what is placed on the agenda.

Let's take a look at some of the commonplace strategies and discern how or why this may or may not be the case.

On a scale from one to twelve, rate your ability (Do you have the knowledge, skills and resources) to accomplish these tasks. 0 = none; 12, means you've got all you need and you need no more.

Then, rate the challenge or the difficulty to accomplish the task. How hard is it? 0 = effortless; 12 = impossible

Task	Ability	Challenge
1. Chairing committee meetings.		
2. Assigning tasks to committee members.		
3. Understanding my responsibilities.		

4. Holding myself accountable as a committee member.		
5. Arriving on time for a meeting.		
6. Finishing meetings on time.		
7. Voicing my opinion in a committee meeting.		
8. Participating without my own personal agenda.		
9. Contributing adequate information for decision-making.		
10. Listening to the stated conversation with intention.		

Where you scored low on ability and high on the challenge: you need more training for the stated expectations and how you can best perform.

When you scored in the middle: you go to meetings to appear responsible but are not a productive contributing member.

When you scored high on ability and low on challenge: you know what needs to be done but no one is giving you a chance to do anything. You are bored to tears and would rather be elsewhere but are probably attending because your boss told you to or you consider it business development. Perhaps, with a little direction you might do more.

Let's reflect on each of these tasks.

1. **Know what's expected.** Chairing effective committee meetings only comes with a clear understanding of what the organization's goals are and how the committee fits into the big picture. A committee chairman's orientation should be provided, separate and apart from a committee orientation.

   It is the responsibility of the Chair to direct the conversation, to make assignments, to record or have recorded a set of action steps, and to hold members accountable for those assignments.

   Good Chairmen set the agendas after reviewing progress with the committee members and the staff liaison.

2. **Assign tasks** evenly and appropriately. Every
   committee should have a separate orientation with
   specific timelines, budgetary constraints and
   ultimate goals.

   Staff members should empower committee
   members to do their jobs. Competent staffs value
   the contributions of volunteers and benefit from
   personal and committee self-growth during the
   process.

3. **Conduct a committee orientation**. If a committee
   member misses said orientation, they should make
   arrangements to make-up that important
   conversation with the Chairman.

   The Committee Chair should know the caliber of
   each and every committee member and what they
   have to contribute to the goals.

4. **Accept responsibility.** Promise what you can
   deliver and deliver with that promise. If the time

constraints are unrealistic, acknowledge that and either ask for more time or release yourself from that pledge. Don't obligate yourself if you can't be dependable.

5. **Start on time**. Celebrate those people who have "followed the rules." Yes, exceptions do happen. Allow yourself a few extra minutes for travel arrangements. Arriving late routinely is rude and inconsiderate.

6. **Finish on time**. With a well-planned agenda and directed conversation, conscientious volunteers will make decisions or defer them until more information is received.

7. **Speak up purposefully**. Would you prefer to be known as the person who talks a lot, or the person who is well respected for what they have to contribute? Ask enough questions so alternatives

can be thoroughly discussed. Introduce best practices or investigate them if you want to learn more.

8. **Leave your personal agenda at the door.** Your role is to do the committee's work, not to foster your own business products and services.

9. **Plan, consider, plan, decide, plan, act, plan, review, plan, review again, plan some more.** Making rash conclusions is often more detrimental than beneficial. In providing adequate time for Murphy's Law during initial planning sessions, all scenarios should have ample discussion before a consensus can be reached.

   Act boldly once decisions have been made.

   Then, review not only once; but twice. The first review is to capture immediate thoughts.

   The second, more thoughtful review is to assure best practices continue and what needs to be tweaked, indeed gets tweaked and tweaked well.

10. **Listen, listen, and listen some more.** When you cross the threshold into a committee meeting, your time belongs to that organization for the good of its constituents. Contribute with that intention in mind. Remember, your privilege to be included comes with the larger responsibility to achieve the organization's goals.

Focus on these words: purposeful, participatory, accountable, dependable, empowering. Are these words that describe your committee meetings or are they aspiring dreams?

HOMEWORK: Which aspects of your board or committee meetings could benefit by using some of these techniques?

Jot down what you can change that will make them more effective.

AFFIRMATION: (Are Y-O-U 100% committed?)

I AM an intentional, focused committee member.

NOTES TO SELF:

GOALS: SMARTE$T

Specific: Who, what, when, where, why and how?	
Measurable: How much, how many?	
Acceptable: to those achieving the goals: attitudes, abilities, skills and $$.	
Realistic: Reflect on previous success and identify optimum conditions to be successful.	
Timely: There is a sense of urgency to accomplish now.	
Extending: Growing the capabilities of those charged with the goals.	
$$$$: What is the cost of accomplishing this goal? What is the cost of not accomplishing this goal?	
Test: Thoroughly appraise any additional changes for each goal through this process. Evaluate for successes and modify if necessary.	

-9-

Rigorous Codes of Ethics and How to Prevail

Whenever you pose the question of ethics, most individuals, organizations or corporations state emphatically, "Oh yes. We have a code of ethics."

Yet, when you think about engaging the code of ethics, and how the codes are actually applied in the workplace, there appears to be a disconnection.

For example, Enron has a 64 page booklet devoted entirely to their ethical procedures. Did anyone ever open it?

Where does one turn to assure that the values and behaviors of the organization are stated, reviewed and enforced? To whom does one turn to foster ethics: your parents, your schools, your legislators, or your community? Do ethics change based on geography, age, occupation, gender or mission?

Aristotle describes ethical virtue as a "hexis" – a tendency or disposition induced by our habits to have appropriate feelings. Further, every ethical virtue is a condition intermediate between two other states, one involving excess, and the other deficiency.

In this respect, Aristotle says," the virtues are no different from technical skills: every skilled worker knows how to avoid excess and deficiency, and is in a condition intermediate between two extremes."

When you translate this into ethical concerns for organizations, let us contemplate the critical principle that differentiates profits from nonprofits and that is: *No one individual should profit from the organization.* That is the defining benchmark.

Some questions to ponder for the development of your organizations' ethics code:

1. How honest are you and your staff? No one expects a grandmother or a new recruit out of school to steal. Did you ask during the interview process, "Do you lie, cheat or steal?" Does anyone spend staff time doing their personal business on the internet? How is that time accounted for on a time sheet?

2. How open are your dealings? Are you afraid to share your board minutes with the general public or the membership? Are your financials posted? Do you have a close knit group of vendors that are related to others serving in some role of leadership? How has that been defined?

3. Do you have a conflict of interest policy and is it signed and acknowledged each year by both your board and your staff? Do you have clear procedures stating what someone should do if they believe that something fishy is occurring even if it's the executive director or the board chair?

4. How is the privacy of your donors, friends, or interested parties protected? Did they consent to having their name published? Do you share your lists? If so, did you get permission in writing to do so?

Let's say that you've got everything written down, passed, documented, reviewed and you are presented with something you weren't prepared for. How would you handle it?

There are many ethical filters: cost-benefit analysis, utilitarian, fairness, consequential, and even more papers written on this topic. (180,000)

The Ethics Resource Center has among others, something called the PLUS model. (www.ethics.org)

"P = Policies; L = Legal; U = Universal and S = Self"

One might use these considerations to debate a particular action. Are there policies in place to handle this situation? If not, why not?

Is it legal? If you have to even question the legality, isn't the message already being delivered?

Is the decision that we are making in alignment with our mission and our guiding principles? How does this activity make me feel personally? Is it something that I am comfortable performing? Or, does it feel just plain icky?

Committing fraud by stating an individual has put in so many hours at work, when they've been conducting personal business on the internet is a very real problem. If they are conducting questionable personal business (porn sites, gambling), there are further complications.

While temptation is there, wouldn't it be clearer for policies to state "no personal business during normal business hours?"

One of the simplest filters for taking action is the light of day test. How would this action appear in tomorrow's headlines? How proud would this make my mom, my dad and my grandmother feel?

No one wants to be the board chair who erroneously decided that the restricted money for the computer programs should be dedicated to a brick walkway or mascot statue. No one wants to be the employee discovering that monies raised by the concession stands have been pilfered by the supervisor.

Rigorous attention to policies, systems for accountability and oversight are required by the smallest of groups. Is yours among them?

HOMEWORK: What can you do to assure that the actions and transactions of your staff, committees and board members are of the highest integrity? What would you have to change? Which board member do you need to champion this initiative?

AFFIRMATION: (Are Y-O-U 100% committed?)

I AM ethical in all of my dealings.

NOTES TO SELF:

GOALS: SMARTE$T

Specific: Who, what, when, where, why and how?	
Measurable: How much, how many?	
Acceptable: to those achieving the goals: attitudes, abilities, skills and $$.	
Realistic: Reflect on previous success and identify optimum conditions to be successful.	
Timely: There is a sense of urgency to accomplish now.	
Extending: Growing the capabilities of those charged with the goals.	
$$$$: What is the cost of accomplishing this goal? What is the cost of not accomplishing this goal?	
Test: Thoroughly appraise any additional changes for each goal through this process. Evaluate for successes and modify if necessary.	

-10-

Engaging Your Board: It's Raining Yen

In 1971, Professor Myles Mace, Harvard Business School, stated, independent directors are "but ornaments on a Christmas tree." With today's fundraising challenges needing more strategic solutions including mergers or dissolutions, it is pertinent that non-decorative board members become focused on them.

Eight out of ten complaints commonly shared by fundraising professionals surround the job of the board to raise funds. Directors of Development query about how to get a non-fundraising board involved in this critical activity. Executive Directors and CEO's report that they aren't meeting fundraising goals and that they don't have a board that thinks this critical function is their job.

Reflect on the skills of your board for a moment and think about the steps you take to engage them in assuring that you have enough money to run your organization.

On a scale from one to twelve, rate your ability (Do you have the knowledge, skills and experience to accomplish these tasks?). 0 = none; 12, means you've got all you need and you need no more.

Then, consider the resources at hand (Do you have the staff, time and money?) and rate the challenge or the difficulty to accomplish the task. How hard is it?. 0 = effortless; 12 = impossible.

Task	Ability	Challenge
1. Assessing the skills of your board to raise funds.		
2. Orienting the board to the concept of fundraising.		
3. Conducting board training for specific aspects of fundraising.		

4. Measuring board fundraising goals.		
5. Reporting on board fundraising activities and goals.		
6. Empowering the board to serve as ambassadors for your organization.		
7. Assigning a committee to determine the needs of our board.		
8. Accepting "right" representation for our board.		
9. Distributing accurate solicitation materials.		
10. Preparing adequate privacy policies for donor management.		

Where you scored low on ability and high on the challenge: you could use a significant shot of courage or training for how you can best support your board and your organization. Ornaments abound!!!

When you score in the middle: you aren't using your board to the best of their ability, despite the fact that you give them the appearance of being responsible. Ornament sighting!

When you score high on ability and low on challenge: Will you ever meet your budget? Ornament alert!

A board committee, be it governance or board development, should be working on the strength of your board each and every year. This may or may not be your nominating committee but whatever you call it, it is the committee of peers that hold others accountable.

It is the board's responsibility to assure a strong fiduciary presence for your mission and a good part of that is raising funds. Every board member must contribute in some way.

Best practices in strong nonprofit organizations include buy-in from every board member. Each individual contributes some gift of monetary significance. This gift should not be "able to be worked off by doing volunteer work." That is a cop out.

Best practices have minimum contributions set and could range from $500 upwards to $10,000 or more.

How is your board holding its members responsible for their obligations?

How do you know what your board members know about your organization, its mission, your agency's position in your community, how respected you are or aren't?

How often do you assess their board skills and do you conduct ongoing training for them on board responsibilities and nonprofit trends?

Can you imagine how it would feel, if you as the chief staff person had 15, 20 or 25 well-versed board members raising money for you and not just appearing as ornaments?

Here's what other chief executives offered as suggestions and success stories with their boards at a recent Main Line Chamber of Commerce Nonprofit Roundtable on this very topic.

> Give specific jobs with specific deadlines. Have clear, crisp goals that are responsible.

> Expand the board. Lead with passionate pocketbooks.

> Find new board members intentionally.

> Conduct training to promote the understanding of their roles.

> De-clutter your board. Permit board business and only board business on the agenda.

> Have THANK YOU events that are socially centered.

> Communicate, communicate, and communicate. Know each board member's preferred method of communication and graciously prepare it for them. Yes, some still prefer to receive snail mail. An e-governance portal may remove hours of frustration from otherwise unproductive board members' performances.

➢ Share a briefing at every board meeting, about what each director has done for the organization since the last meeting.

➢ When you conduct the Strategic Planning session, have board "extras" there (additional committee members, key stakeholders)

Your organization deserves a working board; not one that believes that because you're nonprofit, money flows like manna from heaven. It can only rain yen, if you are purposeful in your actions to meet your fundraising goals.

Close your eyes and imagine this: a fully engaged board, intentionally raising money. Any organization will benefit from operating from a place of abundance. It will do wonders for your organization.

Open your eyes: MAKE IT HAPPEN!

HOMEWORK: What are the training needs of your board members? How do you know this to be true? How will you determine what their needs are?

Identify your own fears that you have about permitting your board to raise funds for you.

AFFIRMATION: (Are Y-O-U 100% committed?)

I AM providing channels for my board members to become stronger in their fund development goals.

NOTES TO SELF:

GOALS: SMARTE$T

Specific: Who, what, when, where, why and how?	
Measurable: How much, how many?	
Acceptable: to those achieving the goals: attitudes, abilities, skills and $$.	
Realistic: Reflect on previous success and identify optimum conditions to be successful.	
Timely: There is a sense of urgency to accomplish now.	
Extending: Growing the capabilities of those charged with the goals.	
$$$$: What is the cost of accomplishing this goal? What is the cost of not accomplishing this goal?	
Test: Thoroughly appraise any additional changes for each goal through this process. Evaluate for successes and modify if necessary.	

-11-

Due Diligence Selecting Your Banking Partner

A huge responsibility for every nonprofit organization is maintaining the public trust given to them by the IRS. Utmost for every board, is their ability to stay on top of their finances.

Yet, reviewing financial reports is often the single activity given the least attention during board meetings.

Which of these types of personalities would you say your board possessed?

The Penny Pincher – can't ever spend any money, because we can't raise the funds. Besides, nonprofits have to look poor or nobody will want to give to them. They'll think we don't need the money.

The Impulsive – My friend did this in Tulsa and made thousands. It's a great idea, we have to do it.

The Magician – Every program that is discussed is adequately funded. We have no money problems or discussions. In addition to our endowments, we have 30% of our annual operating budget in reserves.

The Entrepreneur – I will work as hard as I can for you to realize this fundraising goal, if you let me.

The Socialite – Who cares if we make any money? Let's have a p-a-r-t-a-ae!

A very simple truth is that while you are typing the personality of your board, no one is typing the personality of your bank.

Let's take a look at some of the strategies you could be using with your board and determine how you might support your board in discerning the palatability of assigning your board the charge of continuing your existing banking relationship.

On a scale from one to twelve, rate your ability (Do you have the knowledge, skills and resources) to accomplish these tasks. 0 = none; 12, means you've got all you need and you need no more.

Then, rate the challenge or the difficulty to accomplish the task. How hard is it? 0 = effortless; 12 = impossible.

Task	Ability	Challenge
1. Acquiring sensible spending habits.		
2. Reducing debt systematically.		
3. Managing risk.		
4. Creating judicious investment policies.		
5. Establishing a "relationship" with our bank.		
6. Representing your organization to the public as a winner.		
7. Attracting donors through your 990.		

8. Identifying money- saving strategies.		
9. Demonstrating proudly, the benefits of using your current bank.		
10. Talking with your bank about a better rate for your "reserve" fund.		

Where you scored low on ability and high on the challenge: you could use a significant shot of courage or training for how you can best support your board and your organization.

When you score in the middle: you aren't contributing to the best of your ability, despite the fact that you give the appearance of being responsible.

When you score high on ability and low on challenge: you know that this needs to be done, but you have too many other priorities and this hasn't risen to the top of your pile.

Yet, what could be more important than who has control of your everyday finances?

Here's what your finance committee should be considering:

1. **Financial Strength** – to determine the potential for longevity of your bank, go to www.bauer.com or www.bankrates.com. John Durso, St. Edmonds Bank, has advised that any bank worth their salt should have a rating of 3 ½ stars or greater.

2. **Earning Power** - Is the bank in question earning any money? Financial reports are readily downloadable on their website and you should be able to detect any downwards or upwards trends. If they are significant enough, or you really want to "pick" this bank, give them a courtesy call.

3. **Longevity** - How long have they been in business? Are they growing? Again, information on their website should provide you with some idea about their stability. If you still aren't sure but you are leading towards them, make that call.

4. **History** - Is it a local bank? Is it a bank that is a result of a single merger or lots of mergers? Regardless of which, does the bank have the hometown feel? How community oriented is the personal philosophy at your branch? Are they visibly making a difference in your neighborhood?

5. **Comparable fees** – Are they competitive? Are the bank's rates negotiable? Are your savings rates similar to a money market account? If not, start asking questions.

6. **Fees** – What are you paying for a so-called no minimum balance?

7. **Lendable** - Compare all of your lending rates should you find yourself in that position. Determine what you need to do to be more attractive financially.

8. **Courage** – Find the courage to truly give this responsibility to your board.

Whether your current banking partner is a de noveau bank, a boutique bank or a longstanding community establishment, it is up to you to factor in their continual care approach.

The simple fact is that presently, fewer banks are reaching out for these kinds of partnerships. Their talk is not being complemented by their walk.

You owe it to yourselves, your constituents and the general public to perform due diligence with whatever money you are handling on a daily basis. For long term financial relationships these exercises become even more critical in our current economy.

HOMEWORK: Do you personally hold any fears or resistances around acquiring money?

What beliefs do you possess that will support your organization in handling money more purposefully?

AFFIRMATION: (Are Y-O-U 100% committed?)

I AM willing to discuss our financial matters with our banking agents.

NOTES TO SELF:

GOALS: SMARTE$T

Specific: Who, what, when, where, why and how?	
Measurable: How much, how many?	
Acceptable: to those achieving the goals: attitudes, abilities, skills and $$.	
Realistic: Reflect on previous success and identify optimum conditions to be successful.	
Timely: There is a sense of urgency to accomplish now.	
Extending: Growing the capabilities of those charged with the goals.	
$$$$: What is the cost of accomplishing this goal? What is the cost of not accomplishing this goal?	
Test: Thoroughly appraise any additional changes for each goal through this process. Evaluate for successes and modify if necessary.	

-12-

From the Beginning: Leading Your Way to Successful Voluntarism

Today's economic setbacks offer a plethora of opportunity for nonprofit organizations. There is a displaced workforce amongst our ranks who have been encouraged by the President and others to "volunteer" and learn new skills.

How nonprofits prepare for this onslaught will make a huge difference in their reaction to the abundance of manpower available for them to embrace.

Management must be on board and understand the value of preparing a comprehensive plan for accepting volunteers into their workplace in order for them to exploit this situation. Following a "strike while the iron is hot" mentality, a chaotic approach to accepting, placing, training, evaluating volunteers as well as minimizing your risk can pose seemingly insurmountable obstacles.

Former Secretary of State General Colin Powell believes that "Leadership is allowing ordinary people to be extraordinary." Is your workplace one that permits volunteers to become amazing?

On a scale from one to twelve, rate your ability (Do you have the knowledge, skills and experience to accomplish these tasks?). 0 = none; 12, means you've got all you need and you need no more.

Then, consider the resources at hand (Do you have the staff, time and money?) and rate the challenge or the difficulty to accomplish the task. How hard is it?. 0 = effortless; 12 = impossible.

Task	Ability	Challenge
1. Prioritizing your volunteer program strategically.		
2. Developing a written volunteer plan.		
3. Training the board and staff for volunteer management.		
4. Allocating funds for volunteer programs.		
5. Using volunteers in all aspects of the organization.		
6. Assessing risk management for volunteers including background checks, when appropriate.		
7. Securing adequate insurance for volunteer programs.		
8. Creating written volunteer job descriptions, policies, procedures and handbooks.		
9. Providing ongoing volunteer training.		
10. Nurturing an environment where volunteers can be celebrated for their unique gifts.		

Where you scored low on ability and high on the challenge? Make the time to heighten your skills.

When you scored "in the middle:" you aren't using your staff or your volunteers to their greatest potential, because you don't even know what it is.

When you scored high on ability and low on challenge: why aren't you doing something about your volunteers right now? What's holding you back?

Consider two organizations from polar extremes. One has provided space for a volunteer to accomplish their work. The individual has gone through an interview, read a job description, provided references and signed a contract.

They have participated in an orientation session and appreciate the importance of their job. They know why the mission is so valuable to the community. They have the supplies they need to do their job and understand what the goal of their specific project is. It is something that they are able to accomplish in a time slot that fits into their availability.

Staff and other volunteers are cordial and engage in conversation and permit them to do their job in a way that benefits everyone. They are thanked each and every time they come into the work space.

Now consider the second group. This volunteer is responding to an ad in a posting for volunteers wanted. It is for an Art Show and Auction. There is no actual job description; a summary implies what the goals are. No intake; no interview; no orientation.

The volunteer shows up and no one knows what this individual is supposed to do.

For a brief time, the volunteer handles the money at the registration table. Then, from across the room, a woman in overalls, (maybe a staff member) indicates that they are needed in another position.

Since they have no replacement, the volunteer waits for someone else to replace them. Time passes, no substitute. The overall person shrieks from across the room for them to leave the position and move elsewhere immediately.

The volunteer politely leaves the registration table and resumes working elsewhere. At the close of the program, money is missing at the front desk. This same volunteer is questioned about her time after she left the table and told never to return by the Executive Director, who just happens to be the person in the overalls.

Which organization do you wish you'd be working for, despite the mission connection?

Sounds extreme? It isn't. This is a first-hand experience of something very close to a situation I encountered when I volunteered three years ago to such a plea for help. I will never be back.

As you sculpt your volunteer programs to be risk-free, compliant, amiable, inviting places to attract the most qualified volunteers possible, think about your options. Unexpected results can happen to good organizations that permit regular folks to shine in their jobs, no matter how small.

If volunteers can be appropriately placed in a job that is meaningful for them, on their terms but fitting your guidelines, you can reap magnificent harvest. The best fruit is those who ripen to become performing board members.

HOMEWORK: When is the last time you thought about your nurturing your volunteers? How much staff time and money is allocated for their training? What benefits are realized by your organization because of the volunteers?

AFFIRMATION: (Are Y-O-U 100% committed?)
I AM mindful of each and every volunteer that serves our organization.

NOTES TO SELF:

GOALS: SMARTE$T

Specific: Who, what, when, where, why and how?	
Measurable: How much, how many?	
Acceptable: to those achieving the goals: attitudes, abilities, skills and $$.	
Realistic: Reflect on previous success and identify optimum conditions to be successful.	
Timely: There is a sense of urgency to accomplish now.	
Extending: Growing the capabilities of those charged with the goals.	
$$$$: What is the cost of accomplishing this goal? What is the cost of not accomplishing this goal?	
Test: Thoroughly appraise any additional changes for each goal through this process. Evaluate for successes and modify if necessary.	

-13-

The Art of Giving

Fundraising, as we have discussed, is a constant for any nonprofit organization. A group of volunteers join together as a board of directors to raise funds for a common cause.

"Art" denotes a set of techniques used by somebody in a particular field that is proficient in that technique. Someone who has mastered the art of fundraising therefore would be proficient.

How are you reaching your fundraising goals this year? Of the 1.7 million nonprofits that were registered with the IRS in 2008, United Way of Southeastern PA had identified that 22,000 were in the greater Delaware Valley region.

So much has happened since 2008 in the economy. The Philadelphia Foundation has predicted dissolutions and mergers; the Economy League released its whitepaper to that effect. (www.tpf.org)

How is your organization faring? Are you barely holding on? Are you thriving?

Here are a few more directed fundraising activities where you may focus your energies.

On a scale from one to twelve, rate your ability (Do you have the knowledge, skills, experience and resources) to accomplish these tasks. 0 = none; 12, means you've got all you need and you need no more.

Then, rate the challenge or the difficulty to accomplish the task. How hard is it? 0 = effortless; 12 = impossible.

Task	Ability	Challenge
1. Implementing a multi-cycle giving campaign. (several times a year)		
2. Obtaining grants from private foundations or the government.		
3. Creating collaborations or partnerships with other NPO's.		
4. Acquiring sponsorships for our special events.		
5. Cultivating our donors towards lifelong giving.		
6. Being recognized for our leadership in the community.		
7. Attracting endowments.		
8. Being a magnet for giving circles.		
9. Using the time and talent of FR volunteers wisely.		
10. Accepting gifts in lieu of cash.		

By now, if you've been following, you know the drill.

Wherever you scored low on ability and high on the challenge, you could use a significant shot of courage or training for how you can best support your board and your organization.

When you scored in the middle: you aren't contributing to the best of your ability, despite the fact that you give the appearance of being responsible.

When you scored high on ability and low on challenge, you know that this needs to be done, but you have too many other priorities.

Folks, if fundraising hasn't risen to the top of your pile yet, when do you expect it to? What are you doing about developing your fundraising plan?

At the Chester County Chamber, in the not too distant past, a panel of esteemed philanthropists presented their tips for "The Art of Giving." Here are some of their recommendations that have great relevancy today.

Beth McGarrigle, Board Chair of the Chester County Fund for Women and Girls, reiterated the importance of recognizing every gift no matter how small or how large in a public way. The cultivation of donors is a steady ongoing activity that is never complete. Permitting people to give at a level that is meaningful for them and acknowledging that donation is crucial.

Frances Sheehan, President and CEO of the Brandywine Health Foundation encouraged, "Perhaps the most important lesson in fundraising is to remember to thank people, not just for their financial contributions, but for their donation of time. An expression of gratitude can come in the form of a personalized thank you note -- whether computer-generated or hand-written, a phone call, recognition at a special event for volunteers or donors, or through nomination of a stand-out individual for an award."

Krys Sipple, Executive Director of The Clinic in Phoenixville, brought along sticky 4x8 pads with corporate information on it and distributed them to the participants as she does with her board members.

During her annual campaign, her board members write their own personalized note to the perspective donors encouraging them to give. Krys emphasized the importance of having strong board support in all fundraising endeavors.

Finally Dolly Wideman-Scott, President, Domestic Violence Center of Chester County, advised the group about the importance of considering time and talent as a valid means of gifting. Some people provide true value through their skills, expertise or time which is equally as important as cash.

On LinkedIn, a question for tips for fundraising in a tough economy in a variety of groups and discussion forums was posed. Among more than 50 respondents, Dean Stenehjem, Foundation/Development Director at Rochester Senior Citizen's Center suggested: "Communicate to your donors what a difference their donations have made for those we serve. Communicate what their future donations will do. Step up awareness of your mission/need!"

One of the most powerful recommendations was Barbra Luce-Turner, Senior Director of Development at Loyola University Medical Center stated: "Take donors at their word when they say that they will give in the future when times get better and maintain a good stream of communication focusing on the mission of your organization—even if they are not giving this year."

Regardless of what the recommendation is, it is clear that relationships and the ability to connect with one individual provides the greatest return for requests for giving. No matter what the size of the organization, it is the personal experience that one has with the mission; that correlation is what drives the gifts.

If you would be interested in receiving a complete list of suggestions from those 50 odd different professionals go to "The Art of Giving" page on my website http://www.engagingyourboard.org, find the Giving page and complete your giving style survey and have your personal assessment interpreted. You will receive the tips in an e-book format upon completion of the interpretation. (Survey, 10 minutes; interpretation, 30 minutes; value, $250. Lasting value: priceless)

HOMEWORK: Perform a giving "audit" on your collateral. How does it speak to the consumer? How are your returns being measured? Are you reaching your goals? Why or why not?

AFFIRMATION: (Are Y-O-U 100% committed?)

I AM vigilant about the nuances of individual giving.

NOTES TO SELF:

GOALS: SMARTE$T

Specific: Who, what, when, where, why and how?	
Measurable: How much, how many?	
Acceptable: to those achieving the goals: attitudes, abilities, skills and $$.	
Realistic: Reflect on previous success and identify optimum conditions to be successful.	
Timely: There is a sense of urgency to accomplish now.	
Extending: Growing the capabilities of those charged with the goals.	
$$$$: What is the cost of accomplishing this goal? What is the cost of not accomplishing this goal?	
Test: Thoroughly appraise any additional changes for each goal through this process. Evaluate for successes and modify if necessary.	

-14-

Your Future Self

Imagine if you will, a time in the not too distant future, when your board is working seamlessly to reach your fundraising goals.

Imagine if you were able to implement all of the recommendations or at least some of the ones that seem logical and affordable and easy to integrate into your system of bringing money into your coffers.

There were many questions posed to you among the chapters in this book. It is up to you to determine the future of you and the organization for which you work.

Hopefully, you now have more choices to act upon or not to act upon than you did before you began.

If your board does not raise funds for you, you have choices. If some of your board raises funds for you, you have choices. If all of your board is raising money for you, but it is not enough, you have choices. And if you have a board that is raising all of the money that you need at this time, you still have choices.

While your future is waiting for you to define it, of one thing I am certain.

Albert Einstein said "You cannot solve problems with the mind that created them." If you do not alter your state of mind to accept opportunities that present themselves, than you will wallow in poverty.

The more that you expect from your board, and the more you provide for them, than the more you will gain.

If you fear success, or aspects of it, you will never attain success. You can never achieve what you will not permit.

Look around you. See what successful people do. Their expectations are high enough to be realized but not too high to never be achieved. Their focus on the good rewards their expectations.

There is much truth in the law of attraction and its intersection with the laws of the universe. We reap what we sow. To attract, you must act.

Take each day and find the gifts that are bestowed upon you.

Take each board member and permit them to do good for you and your organization with the gifts that have been bestowed upon them. Your board can become engaged in ways that are most meaningful to themselves and to others.

If you need to effect change, find the champion or champions who will help you. When you are able to allow directed thoughts, words and deeds to accomplish your expectations, you will be successful.

Acknowledge what you have and find the willingness to do more. Bring your champions with you and share the successes that you deserve.

To attract, you must act! To have the skies open up and rain yen (or abundance), you must engage your board.

FINAL EXERCISES: Ask yourself these questions in the first person using I, my, me, our etc.

1. Which recommendations have been implemented? Which, have not?

2. What are the potential **obstacles** that stand between my goals and the fundraising goals for our organization?

3. What will it take to implement any needed change?

4. When I think of **solutions**, am I suspending a limiting belief that I have held? If so, which one?

5. What course of action do I need to take to squelch my own saboteurs?

6. How will I turn my beliefs around to be more successful?

7. Who is on my support team or what is the support system that will guide me through these changes?

8. With whom can I collaborate?

9. Are there skilled professionals that can strengthen my intent?

10. With whom will I celebrate my successes?

11. Lastly, if time and money did not matter, where would I be, what would I be doing and who would I be doing it with?

When you have completed your answers, send them to me at: Kayte@engagingyourboard.org and receive an abbreviated e-book on "Setting Goals for 2011 and Beyond."

Engaging Your Board is part of the *What Helps Leaders Grow* experience. Here is an excerpt from a blog entry from the overall theme of the "Essentials of Modern Leadership" programs another complementary service.

While others Falter

"... Hmmm...'How much had the board raised during the capital campaign? Were they exploring grants? What were their primary sources of funding? How about their annual campaign? Do they have volunteers? Where had they posted the job? What was the board doing? Had he contacted...?' and I began to offer some of the nonprofit fundraiser placement services when he cut me off.

His tone changed. 'The board did NOT want someone who would come in and tell them what to do. The board wanted to HIRE someone to raise the money.' They needed someone who could knock on doors along the Main Line and bring folks in to give his organization (located at the opposite end of the spectrum of the Main Line, geographically as well as philosophically), the funds they needed.

'Did I know someone who was QUALIFIED to do that? Who could raise $100,000 and their own salary in three months?' No, sadly I did not. If I knew someone who could, I don't think I would have offered them up as a sacrificial lamb to another good organization led astray by misguided board members...."

For the complete blog and to subscribe, go to:

http://blog.essentialsofmodernleadership.com/2010/10/0
4/while-others-falter.aspx

About the Author

Kayte Connelly, CCT is an award winning author, leadership coach and organizational development consultant.

She has over 25 years of experience in community leadership and has worked in business, education, with special populations, government and the arts. Connelly has acted as a successful change agent, designing systems that assist individuals and their organizations in dreaming big and accomplishing those dreams.

Where are you now? Where do you want to be? What's in the way?

A "cultivator", Connelly works with individuals who want more for their business and personal lives and who are interested in leaving a legacy of leadership in their wake. She serves on numerous boards and committees throughout the

MidAtlantic region and was a regular contributor to the Philadelphia Women's Journal.

She can be reached at **Kayte@engagingyourboard.org**.

Best Principled Solutions LLC is a full service governance and leadership coaching and consulting practice and conducts work virtually as well as in person. For more information or to subscribe to her FREEZINE, go to:
www.bestprincipledsolutions.com
www.engagingyourboard.org
http://blog.essentialsofmodernleadership.com

Index

Communication, 57, 115, 146

Confidentiality, 46, 54

Conflict of Interest, 54, 67, 103

Control, 3, 90, 123

E

Ethics, 7, 100, 101, 102, 104

Evidence, 27, 37

Expectations, 3, 7, 30, 31, 40, 44, 57, 63, 70, 73, 80, 91, 153

F

Fiduciary, 4, 7, 11, 43, 47, 52, 113

Fundraising, 4, 42, 47, 71, 110, 111, 112, 116, 121, 140, 141, 143, 144, 145, 151, 155

G

Goal, 13, 23, 25, 31, 35, 51, 62, 77, 88, 99, 109, 119, 121, 129, 133, 139, 150

H

Homework, 9, 11, 23, 33, 49, 60, 75, 86, 97, 107, 117, 127, 137, 148

I

IBP™, 63, 68, 71, 72

Intention, 39, 91, 96

IRS, 1, 10, 120, 140

L

Leadership, 7, 26, 27, 79, 131, 156

M

MasterStream®, 3

Mission, 1, 4, 8, 9, 10, 11, 38, 39, 40, 44, 46, 66, 67, 81, 84, 101, 104, 113, 114, 133, 135, 146

P

Permission, 2, 3, 18, 70, 71, 103

Philanthropy, 143

Policy, 7, 47, 52, 53, 68, 82, 103

Procedures, 54, 85, 100, 103, 132

Process, 13, 25, 35, 39, 43, 44, 51, 58, 62, 63, 67, 68, 72, 77, 88, 93, 99, 102, 109, 119, 129, 139, 150

Productive/ity, 3, 7, 28, 72, 89, 91

CPSIA information can be obtained at www.ICGtesting.com
Printed in the USA
BVOW030528230413

318856BV00001B/2/P